THE MAGNA CARTA

RICHARD BARRINGTON & EDMUND BARRINGTON

Britannica
Educational Publishing

IN ASSOCIATION WITH

ROSEN
EDUCATIONAL SERVICES

Published in 2017 by Britannica Educational Publishing (a trademark of Encyclopædia Britannica, Inc.) in association with The Rosen Publishing Group, Inc.
29 East 21st Street, New York, NY 10010

Distributed exclusively by Rosen Publishing.
To see additional Britannica Educational Publishing titles, go to rosenpublishing.com.

First Edition

Britannica Educational Publishing
J.E. Luebering: Executive Director, Core Editorial
Mary Rose McCudden: Editor, Britannica Student Encyclopedia

Rosen Publishing
Jacob R. Steinberg: Editor
Nelson Sá: Art Director
Nicole Russo: Designer
Cindy Reiman: Photography Manager
Bruce Donnola: Photo Researcher

Library of Congress Cataloging-in-Publication Data

Names: Barrington, Richard, author. | Barrington, Edmund, author.
Title: The Magna Carta / Richard Barrington & Edmund Barrington.
Description: New York : Britannica Educational Pub. in association with Rosen Educational Services, 2017. | Series: Let's find out! primary sources | Includes bibliographical references and index.
Identifiers: LCCN 2016020465| ISBN 9781508103943 (library bound : alk. paper) | ISBN 9781680486063 (pbk. : alk. paper) | ISBN 9781508103189 (6-pack : alk. paper)
Subjects: LCSH: Magna Carta—Juvenile literature. | Constitutional history—England—To 1500—Juvenile literature.
Classification: LCC KD3948 .B37 2017 | DDC 342.4202/9—dc23
LC record available at https://lccn.loc.gov/2016020465

Manufactured in China

Photo credits: Cover, p. 1 Bettmann/Getty Images; p. 4, 28 © AP Images; p. 5 Encyclopædia Britannica, Inc.; pp. 6, 18 © Photos.com/Thinkstock; pp. 8, 27 WPA Pool/Getty Images; p. 9 Robert Alexander/Archive Photos/Getty Images; p. 10 Heritage Images/Hulton Fine Art Collection/Getty Images; p. 11 Universal Images Group/Getty Images; p. 12 Popperfoto/Getty Images; p. 14 Photo © Tallandier/Bridgeman Images; p. 15 Universal History Archive/Universal Images Group/Getty Images; pp. 17, 19 From The British Library/PD; p. 20 © PjrTravel/Alamy Stock Photo; p. 21 Simon Booth/Shutterstock.com; p. 22 © f8 archive/Alamy Stock Photo; p. 23 INTERFOTO/Alamy Stock Photo; pp. 24, 25 Culture Club/Hulton Archive/Getty Images; p. 26 Library of Congress, Washington, D.C. (digital file no. 3g09904u); p. 29 Paul Daniels/Shutterstock.com; interior pages background image Tischenko Irina/Shutterstock.com.

CONTENTS

Making the Rules for a Country

The Magna Carta is an 800-year-old document. Only four copies of the original document exist today.

What would happen if there were no rules? It may sound like fun because it means you could do whatever you wanted. But without rules, people could also steal or hurt each other and not be punished. People would be unsafe, and life would not be fair. Rules help protect people.

All modern governments have sets of rules called laws.

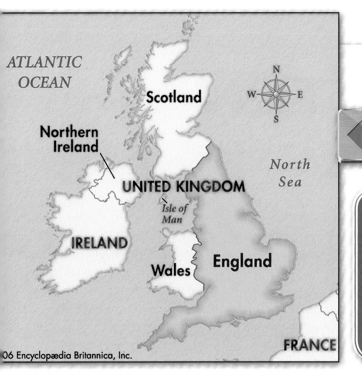

The Magna Carta was signed in England. It created laws for that country.

These laws are usually written down so that everybody knows what they are. Governments did not always have written rules. One of the first examples in history of a government's written laws is the Magna Carta (Latin for "Great **Charter**"). This document was signed more than 800 years ago in England.

The story of the Magna Carta involves a disliked king and rebellious nobles. Keep reading to learn about how the Magna Carta was created and how countries like the United States studied it to make their own laws.

A WRITTEN RECORD

The Magna Carta was a document that gave certain rights to the English people. Putting those rights down in writing

King John of England signed the Magna Carta in 1215.

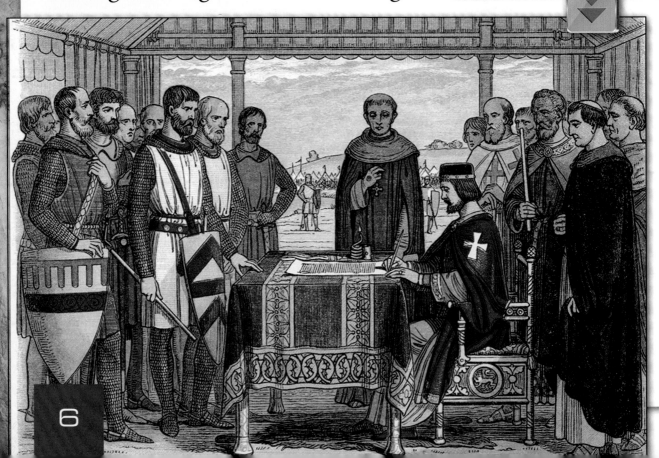

THINK ABOUT IT

Think about what rules you have to follow at home and at school. Which rules make you safer? Which rules would you change if you could, and why?

was important for two reasons. First, the Magna Carta created an agreement between the king of England and his people. By writing down the laws, everyone knew what the laws were. People could point to the written laws if a disagreement came up. The Magna Carta meant that the king could no longer make up new laws whenever he wanted. Instead, even the king had to follow the rules written in the Magna Carta. It was the first document to state that citizens had rights.

The second reason why it was important that the laws of the Magna Carta were written down is that it gives historians a primary source to study. After 800 years, how else would historians today know how England's government worked back in 1215? We would

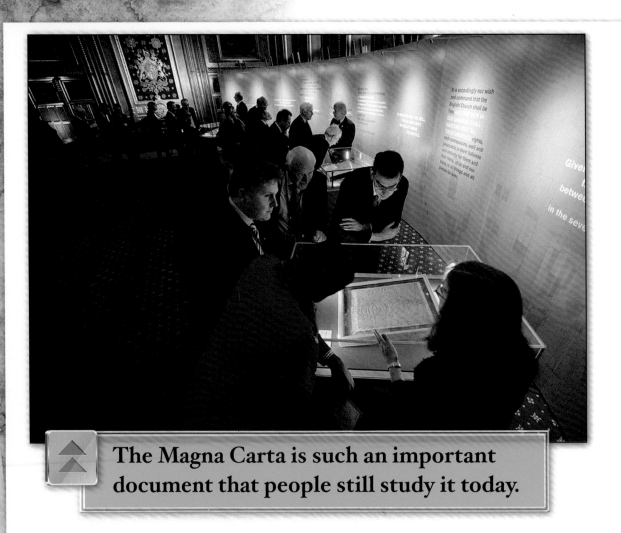

The Magna Carta is such an important document that people still study it today.

only know about England's early laws and history from stories that were retold over time. When people tell stories instead of writing things down, there can be several versions of what really happened. Sadly, many

Primary sources are writings or other sources of firsthand information that date back to the time or event being studied. Because there are still four copies of the original Magna Carta today, we can study the actual words as they were written in 1215.

things would be forgotten. With the Magna Carta and other **primary sources,** we have a more objective idea of what really happened.

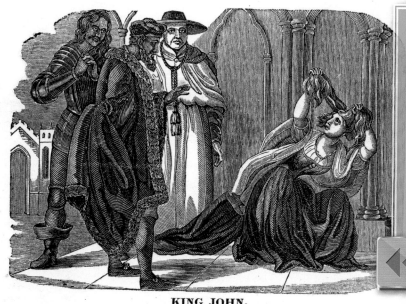

KING JOHN.
Act III.—Scene 4.

William Shakespeare's play *King John*, written in the 1600s, is a secondary source.

Kings and Nobles

In the 1200s, England was an **absolute monarchy**. From 1199 until 1216, it was ruled by King John. As king, John could declare whatever laws he wanted. He made English people fight in many wars and collected taxes from the people to pay for them.

At that time, England also had a social system called feudalism. Under feudalism, powerful people called nobles or lords built large

As king of England, John had unlimited power.

estates and protected people who lived on their land. In return, the people the nobles protected, called serfs, farmed the nobles' land. The king of a country protected all the nobles. The nobles provided money and services to the king to pay him for protection.

Without written laws or rights for the people living in England, King John could treat the English nobles (called barons) badly. The barons could also treat the people who worked for them badly, too.

KING JOHN

King John was born in 1167 in England. When his brother Richard died in 1199, John became king of England. England's barons, church leaders, and the common people disliked John. He demanded a lot of money from them in the form of taxes. He

King John was disliked by many of England's barons and by leaders of the Catholic Church.

also argued with the leaders of the Roman Catholic Church, which was very powerful in England at the time.

THINK ABOUT IT

Think about nobles living under feudalism. Why do you think nobles would support a king who decided to go to war? What are some reasons they would not support him?

One reason John demanded high taxes from his people was for a series of wars he fought with France. In 1200, John married a French woman named Isabella. However, Isabella was supposed to marry a French noble named Hugh IX of Lusignan. (The Lusignans were a French noble family.) This made the Lusignans angry. To settle the matter, John was ordered to appear before King Philip II of France. When John failed to appear, Philip II declared a war to take John's land in France.

Wars are expensive. Under the feudal system, the English barons had to provide money and troops to John. However, John kept demanding more money and

During John's reign, the English fought and lost expensive wars in France.

troops from the barons. By 1206, John had lost several territories that he had held in France. The barons became angry that they were losing money and troops.

In a monarchy, the people do not vote for their rulers. Kings and queens inherit their power. The people support them because they are strong, powerful leaders.

However, after France defeated England, John looked weak. Several years into John's reign, the barons lost their patience with the king. They were ready to demand changes.

Led by Robert Fitzwalter (*pictured here*), the barons demanded that John change.

15

SIGNING THE MAGNA CARTA

How could the barons limit John's power? They were tired of paying such high taxes. They could have fought a war against John to take away his power. However, these nobles were already tired of spending money and sending troops to fight wars. Waging war against the king would cost them even more money. They did not want to fight unless they had to.

Instead of trying to remove John from power, the barons wrote a list of rules and rights. They wanted John

THINK ABOUT IT

If the barons had simply replaced John with another king, do you think that would have fixed their problems? Think about why having a different king, but no list of rules, could have been just as bad.

to follow the rules, which would limit his power. They also wanted him to respect their rights. This list of laws and rights was the Magna Carta.

The barons knew John would not agree to the Magna Carta unless he had no choice. So a group of barons began a

The Articles of the Barons was a list of demands that became the basis for the Magna Carta.

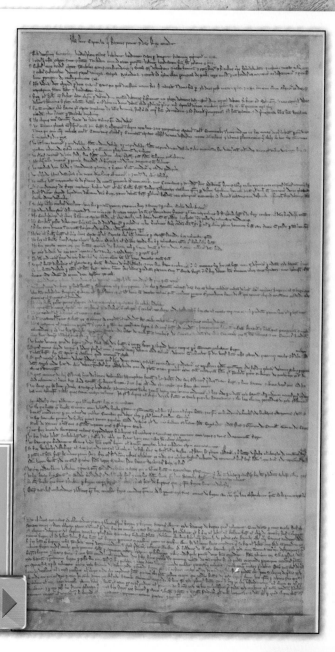

John was forced to sign the Magna Carta in June 1215.

VOCABULARY

A **rebellion** is an organized effort by a group of people to change the government or leader of a country.

rebellion against him. John did not like what the Magna Carta said, but he was too weak to resist the barons. If John did not sign the Magna Carta, the barons would overthrow him. So John agreed to sign the

charter. He signed the document at Runnymede on the River Thames in June 1215. However, John continued to fight the barons, and the dispute led to a civil war. John died in October 1216, in the midst of the civil war.

A civil war broke out between John and the barons in 1215.

The Magna Carta became the basis for English law. It had sixty-three sections called clauses. These clauses were meant to protect the rights of the church and the English barons. However, the ideas in the Magna Carta reached beyond England. Many other countries used the Magna Carta to help form their own laws.

FREEDOM OF THE CHURCH

The first clause of the Magna Carta deals with the freedom of the church. During his reign, John tried to tell the leaders of the Roman Catholic Church in England how the church should be run. Often the church leaders disagreed with John. John punished them by taking their property and money.

Archbishop Stephen Langton played an important role in securing the freedom of the church.

In clause 1, the Magna Carta says, "The English church shall be free, and shall have its rights undiminished and its liberties unimpaired." This means the government could not take away any of the church's rights or its freedoms. The king could no longer take the church's money for his own uses.

This clause did not apply to King John only. The clause says that the church's freedom will exist "for us and our heirs for ever." In other words, the rights listed in the Magna Carta were meant to last forever.

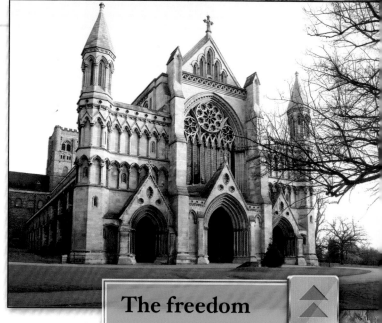

The freedom of the church in England has lasted to this day.

THINK ABOUT IT

Why shouldn't the government be allowed to take money from the church?

LIMITING TAXES

One of the king's most important powers before the Magna Carta was that he could demand any taxes he wanted from his people. However, clause 12 of the Magna Carta says, "No scutage or aid shall be imposed in our kingdom unless by common counsel of our kingdom..." ("Scutage" and "aid" refer to taxes.) This

The Magna Carta meant that kings could no longer collect taxes without the barons' approval.

COMPARE AND CONTRAST
Clause 1 of the Magna Carta gives the church certain freedoms, but clause 12 deals with the barons' rights. How are the two clauses different? What do they have in common?

means the barons had to agree that taxes were fair. If they didn't, the king could not collect the money.

Clause 14 explains how the barons and church leaders will decide if taxes are fair or not. Clauses 12 and 14 became the basis for the idea of the Parliament, the group in England's government that makes the country's laws.

Shown is a meeting of an early form of Parliament.

THE RIGHT TO JUSTICE

Before the Magna Carta, the king could arrest and punish anybody he wanted. Several clauses of the Magna Carta protect people from being arrested or punished for no reason.

Clause 20 says that a person can only be punished "in accordance with the degree of the offence." This means a person could not be sent to jail for a long time or put to death for a small crime. Furthermore, clause 38 says that a person

Before the Magna Carta, punishments were often cruel and unfair.

THINK ABOUT IT

Why do you think it is important for there to be witnesses to a crime before somebody is put on trial?

cannot be put on trial without "reliable witnesses" who can give evidence.

Clause 39 is one of the most important clauses in the charter. It says, "No free man shall be arrested or imprisoned...except by the lawful judgment of his peers." This means that a person could not be sent to prison unless a group of people like him or her all agreed that the person actually committed the crime.

After the Magna Carta, prisoners could not be sent to jail without a trial.

LIVING HISTORY

The Magna Carta may be more than 800 years old, but it is more than just a part of history. Many of its clauses influenced laws that still exist today. The American **Founding Fathers** used it as a model for many of the rights and laws they made for the United States.

VOCABULARY

The United States' **Founding Fathers** were the most important political leaders during the American Revolution and the formation of the United States. They included Benjamin Franklin, Thomas Jefferson, and George Washington, among others.

Ideas from the Magna Carta influenced how the U.S. government was formed.

Today, England is part of the United Kingdom. The country is still a monarchy, but thanks to the ideas in the Magna Carta, the powers of its king or queen are limited. The people of England vote for some members of the country's Parliament, who help make the laws. Other members of Parliament are nobles and church leaders.

In the 1700s, the Founding Fathers put many of the same rights that are in the Magna Carta into the U.S. Constitution. The basic rights of individual citizens, including the right to a fair trial, were taken from the

Today, the English monarch's power is limited by an elected Parliament.

LINCOLN KING JOHN
MAGNA CARTA 1215

A visitor at the U.S. Library of Congress looks at a copy of the Magna Carta.

Magna Carta and written into the Bill of Rights.
Not only have the ideas in the Magna Carta survived

THINK ABOUT IT

Think about how the United Kingdom and the United States might be different if the Magna Carta had never been signed.

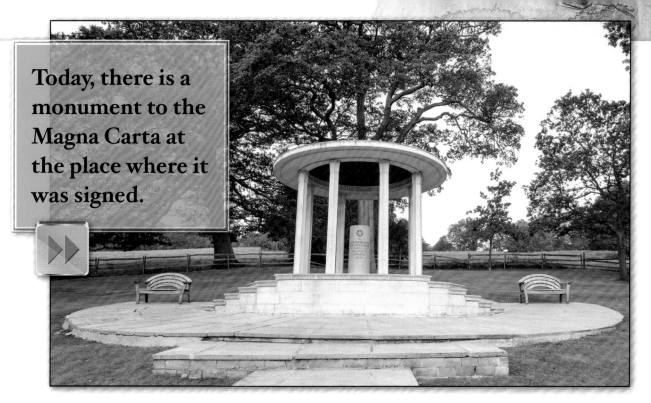

Today, there is a monument to the Magna Carta at the place where it was signed.

for more than 800 years, but so have four copies of the original document. These copies are protected carefully so that they survive for many more years.

In 2015, the four surviving original copies of the Magna Carta were brought together for the 800th anniversary of its signing. They were displayed in the British Parliament building. Because of the important rights and freedoms it created, people will study the Magna Carta for years to come.

GLOSSARY

constitution A document listing the main laws of a country or group, including the powers of the government and the rights of the people.

counsel Advice given to someone.

document A written or printed paper giving information about or proof of something.

evidence Material presented to a court to help find the truth in a matter.

firsthand Coming directly from the original source.

government A group that creates laws and runs a country or region.

historian A student or writer of history.

inherit To receive (for example, money, property, or a title) from someone when that person dies.

law A rule put in place by the government that requires people to act in a certain way.

liberties Freedoms of an individual or group.

monarchy A form of government that has a single person known as a monarch at its head.

noble Somebody who has a high rank in society, usually because of that person's family.

objective Based on facts rather than feelings or opinions.

overthrow To remove (someone or something) from power, especially by force.

parliament The unit of some governments that passes laws for the country.

reign The authority or rule of a monarch.

rights Types of behavior that people in a country are allowed.

serfs People in the past who belonged to a low social class and who lived and worked on land owned by another person.

taxes Money that people are charged to pay the expenses of their government.

FOR MORE INFORMATION

Books

Baxter, Roberta. *The Magna Carta: Cornerstone of the Constitution*. Chicago, IL: Heinemann Library, 2012.

Cameron, Eileen. *Rupert's Parchment: Story of Magna Carta*. Herndon, VA: Mascot Books, 2015.

Lloyd, Christopher, and Patrick Skipworth. *The Magna Carta Chronicle: Eight Hundred Years in the Fight for Freedom*. Tonbridge, UK: What On Earth Books, 2015.

Owen, Ruth. *The Life of a Medieval Knight*. St. Austell, UK: Ruby Tuesday Books, 2014.

Peach, L. du Garde. *King John and Magna Carta*. London, UK: Penguin, 2016.

Steele, Denise Elaine Conquest. *The Mystery of the Magna Carta*. Leicester, UK: Troubador, 2016.

Websites

Because of the changing nature of internet links, Rosen Publishing has developed an online list of websites related to the subject of this book. This site is updated regularly. Please use this link to access the list:

http://www.rosenlinks.com/LFO/carta

INDEX